A Teenager in Lockdown

A Survivor's Story

Favour B-Wilson

contained within this document, including, but not limited to, errors, omissions, or inaccuracies.

Praise, Reviews & Endorsements

In the time of recent trials, we as older persons often look towards the experience, we have had of a changing world to help us. In this experience, we too often rely on ourselves and in doing so often overlook the fact that young people and their peer group as teenagers do not have that history of experience to draw on and therefore must become self-reliant in not only a world of COVID-19 but also that of Social Media.

In such a world I have sat down with my own teenage granddaughter and would now implore all to look back to the juncture when we started out and rejoice in the new generation coming forward and listen to them as they "try to put down in words the beginning of their journey along with their trial and tribulations" I feel sure that her thoughts will resonate with that of many other teenagers.

Chief Robert M Garrioch Nwanni Di Nambe the 1st of Enugu Ammurri. United Kingdom

---

Having taken the time to commit her thoughts and experiences to paper in her new book, I believe that by sharing her personal experiences of lockdown Favour will be a welcome light and helpful resource for many teenage children. It is vital that we help children realise that their experiences are not unusual, and they have not been alone in facing the challenges of 2020! Well done Favour.

Jim Grimmer – Scotland, United Kingdom

Miss Favour Balogun-Wilson captured the unprecedented urgency of the pandemic invasion of our livelihood like a snapshot. She exhibited a spectacular brilliance that should be nurtured and cherished.

Dr Boma Douglas - Chairman at Central Association of Nigerians in the UK (**CANUK**). England, United Kingdom.

Favour demonstrated throughout her book, the power of impactful network with intentionality. Kudos for your gift of authentic narratives, I recommend this book.

Dr Remi Duyile - Ex V.P Bank of America, President & CEO, Image Consulting Group. Distinguished Professor, banker, and entrepreneur. (USA).

All over the world COVID 19 has impacted lifestyles especially with the lockdown. The wonderful book written by this 14-year-old will help others to navigate the new normal lifestyle to an advantage to ensure total well-being and resilience for all. The book is a must-read.

Professor Sidi Osho - Pioneer & Past Vice-Chancellor, Afe Babalola University & President/Founder of Sidi Osho Foundation.

Uncharted waters can be unsettling, bringing cheers and fears. In crossing from one year into a new one, fireworks were invented in China to supposedly ward off evil spirit while the Babylonians made new year resolutions and vows to appease their gods. Such acts were an attempt to make an unknown future secure. In life, the question is not if lockdowns will come, but when and how long! Sometimes we have advance notice, but usually not!! "A Teenager in Lockdown" gives some recipe for the unknown future.

Dr O. Komolafe – Glasgow, United Kingdom.

Miss Favour Balogun-Wilson has written one of the first books to guide us (especially young people) through the ups and downs of living in the first lockdown of this generation. I am sure this will be a delightful guide full of important information for those who want to enjoy the story of how a teenager spent her time during the COVID-19 lockdown in the UK. More importantly, it's a must-read because Covid-19 has now changed the way we live forever.

It is not surprising that Favour has spent her time documenting what she did during the lockdown, she is from a family where giving is a way of life. I recommend this book.

Chief Bimbo Roberts Folayan - CEO of Nigerian Diaspora Direct Investment Summit (NDDIS).

In this book, Favour takes us through her thoughts and feelings during the pandemic, giving an insightful and interesting journey of what has happened to many young people that lived through this difficult time.

Dr Yazan Masannat, MBBS, MRCS(Ed), MRCSI(Dublin), DBRM(UAB), FEBS (Breast Surgery), FRCSEd (Gen Surgery), MD(Leeds)

Miss Favour Balogun-Wilson in this unique book entitled "A Teenager in Lockdown" has demonstrated her exceptional intelligence, impactful character, and depth of knowledge. The narratives in the book are clear, genuine and educative. The content of the book demonstrates her gift of authenticity as clearly documented in all the narratives.

As the Chairman/CEO of Nigerians In Diaspora Commission (NiDCOM), I am excited that not only is our first generation diasporans making us proud but also the second and third generations, as exemplified by Favour in this unique book.

I enjoin Nigerian youths to judiciously use their time effectively in such a way that it will have positive impact on humankind.

Once again, I congratulate Favour on this book and I wish her more successes ahead.

Hon. Abike Dabiri-Erewa - Chairman / CEO Nigerians in Diaspora Commission (NIDCOM)

Miss Favour Balogun-Wilson experienced tough times during the COVID-19 pandemic lockdown, the bonding with her family members through the weeks of this lockdown brought her to maturity and she was able to cope with life despite all odds.

This book is a must read by all teenagers and parents alike to enable them to learn how to cope with confinement in the 21st century. Parents too will learn how to provide a supportive environment for their children with special talents.

Brigadier General (Rtd) S W Aliu – Director of Administration, Army Command & Nigerian Army Officers' Wives Association (NAOWA) Hospital

In this book entitled **'A Teenager in Lockdown'**, the author, Miss Favour Balogun-Wilson, has been able to display her exceptional creativity, innovation, and intelligence. The narratives in the book are relatable, concise and truly educative, focusing on what we all have been through in the uncertain time of the novel COVID-19 pandemic.

By this feat from this teenager, it is pleasing to note that even the second and third generation Nigerians of Diaspora parents are making their mark globally, in line with the vision to encourage them to do exploits and bring honour back home.

The book is indeed a testimony to the fact that as leaders, our message to the Diaspora to continue to seek glory, is resonating well with our overseas-based compatriots.

I hereby endorse and recommend the book to everyone, as I am convinced it will have a positive impact on our collective experience.

Once again, I congratulate Miss Favour on this timely book and wish her more successes in her future endeavours.

H.E. Dr Goodluck Ebele Jonathan GCFR, GCON - President Federal Republic of Nigeria (2010-2015)

Dedication and Acknowledgement

I dedicate this book to my parents who encouraged me to pursue my dreams and never give up. I also want to thank my brothers and friends who inspired this book. Finally, I want to dedicate this book to every teenager out there whose lives have been impacted by COVID-19. I hope that this book will let you know that you are not alone with whatever struggles you might be facing because of the pandemic.

This book is a written adaptation of my experience. Apart from the author's name, all other names have been modified to protect the identities and privacy of the individuals. The school and residential locations have also been slightly modified.

Table of Contents

Chapter 1:
The Beginning

The Earth was in pain
Floods, earthquakes and fires occurred
Rainfall was either too little or too much
Impacts of global warning were ignored
Then along came COVID.

Suddenly, we were forced to listen
To the Earth's groans and aches
Our deafness to the Earth suddenly disappeared
With our attention on full alert
When COVID came along.

It is not impossible to see
That we were united at war with an invisible enemy
Our strategy changing with each passing day
Leaders trying to keep everyone safe
All because COVID came along.

For me, it all began on 16 March 2020. We had just finished maths class when the news came in that the prime minister of the United Kingdom had announced that the whole country would be going into lockdown from Monday 23 March 2020. No one could visit another household. Everyone was to maintain a two-metre distance from each other, and we were not allowed to travel more than five miles from our homes. The only time you could go out was for daily exercise and essential food shopping. At the time, I had no idea of the real impact of this news. At this point, my teenage mind couldn't possibly grasp what we were about to experience. The reason for all this was because a new disease, called Covid-19, had very suddenly become a pandemic.

It had started in Wuhan, the capital of Central China's Hubei Province. The news filled up with reports of illness, deaths, panic and tests. At this point, I felt like someone trapped in a bad dream. I kept replaying the news over and over in my head. The thought of how one virus could cause so much global damage, pain and disruption was unnerving. I once read somewhere that the mental damage caused by trauma could be as devastating as physical damage. That was what this felt like – the virus was having a damaging effect on my mental health without even infecting me physically. It felt like my brain was so filled up that I couldn't even focus on simple things like reading a book or going to school. Every waking moment seemed to be consumed with thinking about the virus. Even my dreams were filled with events and conversations about the virus. I had no idea at this point that more turmoil was to come.

I asked some of our teachers what the plan was for the last two weeks of the school term. They had no idea but kept reassuring me that it would be all sorted before 23 March. Then my answer finally came. A special assembly was called for all the students. I remember walking into the hall and taking my spot, as I would have done with all other assemblies, but from all indications, this one was different. Usually, we had themes or certain groups of students or staff members taking assembly; however, once we were all settled down, just the headmistress walked in and mounted the podium. Immediately there was silence, as we didn't often have her taking assemblies. She began with the usual 'Good day' and the announcements – nothing out of the ordinary. Then, the moment came: 'I'm afraid there is a global pandemic which will affect us all.' She said. By now, you could hear a pin drop in that vast expanse of a school assembly hall. Then, as if on cue, murmurs arose and confusion crossed our faces. It was at this moment, the pandemic became real to me, not just a rumour but, in fact, today's reality. The virus was now present in our nation and causing deadly havoc. Once we'd quietened down again, the headmistress went on to say that we would be spending the last two weeks of school at home while learning virtually. She assured us that our parents had been informed and plans had been put in place to make the transition to virtual learning seamless.

It was difficult to concentrate on the rest of the day's lessons because of this gloomy news. By the time I got to the final class of the day, I was completely distracted. The biology lesson on nutrition was lost on me, and I was glad when school came to an end. As I walked home with my friends, Lucy, Kimberly, Josh and Peter, we discussed how the lockdown was going to impact us individually and what it would mean for the world. Our greatest concern was how our parents were going to react to the lockdown. One thing our parents had in common was obeying the law, so we knew for certain that any plans to meet up or hang out and go shopping together were now suspended. We made a pact to hold a FaceTime chat every day at 4 p.m. to check up on each other.

As per the headmistress's announcement, school duly closed, and we had to finish the rest of the term at home. 'Home-schooling' became a household phrase. I was filled with horror at the thought of being around my family every minute of my day. Images of being hunched over a computer and receiving lessons from my teachers while my parents hovered in the background ran through my mind. You see, my school was a place that I could escape from home and be a fun-loving teenager without being reminded of the responsibilities of doing house chores, keeping an eye on Freddie or tidying up my room. The six-plus hours at school from Monday to Friday, including the hours hanging out with friends, created the social balance away from immediate family that any normal teenager craves.

I got home that afternoon and, sure enough, my parents were planning the family lockdown strategy. Dad had arrived home earlier that day, having had to cut short a business trip. As my parents were not key workers, we did not qualify to continue to attend school, so mum was trying to organise how my brothers and I would be set up to learn while she and dad worked from home. I could tell that a lot of effort was going into making the arrangement work for all of us. A shopping list of major essentials was drafted, and input from us kids was sought. I wanted a big bag of sweets and snacks as I thought a stash would be a necessity to help us cope during the uncertain times ahead. At this stage, I had not given much thought to the set up for learning or how long the lockdown was going to last. Reports of the scarcity of wipes, toilet rolls, hand sanitiser, hand wash, flour and tinned foods were all over the news. The lockdown was making people behave as if aliens were invading the planet and we were all going to be hiding in a bunker. My anxiety levels suddenly increased with all the panic buying and lockdown.

My parents did a great job stocking up the house with food, snacks and essential household items. Interestingly, mum refused to panic-buy things that were scarce. She kept insisting that there was no sense to it all, food shops were staying open, and there never was a pronouncement about stores being closed. She did not like the pictures of bare shelves and NHS workers not being able to buy essentials after a hard day's work. 'If people only bought what they needed, there would be enough to go around,' she said to justify her argument. Mum was never a great lover of shopping, so I was not sure at first if she was just saying this to avoid doing a massive shopping expedition that would require her to traipse from store to store. She would always make a list and stick to a budget. She hates wasting food or impulse buying. 'People are starving all around the world. Wasting food is taking your privilege for granted,' she would always say to us whenever we took more than we could eat and left food on our plates. Her logic about not stocking up on those essentials turned out to be right.

My parents were doing everything possible to get my brothers and me to understand the impact of the pandemic and the rules set out by the government. The importance of staying indoors and washing our hands each time we left or returned home was drummed into our ears constantly. Even though we only went out for family walks, washing our hands was still considered necessary as dad said we may have unwittingly touched a surface contaminated with the virus. I often contemplated how this was possible on a two- or three-mile walk where no sitting or standing was involved. My four-year-old brother, Freddie, taught all of us to sing 'Happy Birthday to You' twice when washing our hands. This was something he had learnt in nursery school that guaranteed washing your hands for at least twenty seconds. I must admit that this injected a bit of fun and humour to the whole hand-washing process. It was even more fun that Freddie took it upon himself to police us washing our hands and singing the song while we did it!

Suddenly, watching the *BBC News at Six* became important for all of us. My parents told us that it would keep us informed and updated on what was happening around the world. I think it must be a generation mindset because you can get the same information on your phone without gathering around the TV. However, I think my parents believed the information would prepare us on how best to manage during the lockdown and were using the daily six o'clock BBC news as an opportunity for us to spend time together as a family. I could not understand what additional preparation would be required. All I kept getting from the news was the number of cases and deaths from Covid-19 and how much the NHS was being stretched beyond capacity. I found the analysis of the virus's behaviour fascinating as I cynically thought the grown-ups were using it to try and show they were on top of it all. The initial assessment that healthy young people could not die from the virus made me wonder if we should even be under lockdown with the adults. I thought we were being trapped at home by the government, who was figuring out how to demonstrate that everything was under control. However, when it became known that young people could be carriers of the virus without showing symptoms, it made more sense to me. I found the 'Help save lives' and 'Protect the NHS' clips on TV and the official announcements interesting because government leaders clearly felt a sense of responsibility to broadcast the message in person in order to convey the weight of its importance. Without a doubt, though, the animated versions got through to me better because they touched my inner child. All the social media platforms I was plugged into also carried the same messages.

Why Africa, being poverty-ridden, was not seeing the spike of Covid-19 cases like the Western world, seemed to baffle the researchers and scientists. I wondered if the fact that the African continent experienced intense sunshine and temperatures of over 50 degrees Celsius had slowed the spread of the virus. Deep down in my heart, I was quite pleased for Africa as I knew the continent had dealt with its fair share of tragedies over the years, including diseases like Ebola, Lassa fever, AIDS and malaria, and did not need Covid-19 to be added to the list. If the virus got hold of the continent as it was gripping countries in the West, the death rates would be high and unmanageable. In a twisted way, I felt the West was equipped with the technology and advancement to come up with a solution swiftly.

As the days passed, the impact of the virus became clearer. Each time I had chats or FaceTime calls with my friends, it seemed to be all we talked about. We compared notes on what our parents were doing. Now we had to be around the house 24/7 without a break from it all. We were not allowed to go out on our own so we would not be tempted to meet up with each other.

The daily exercise encouraged by the government was being taken seriously by our parents. We had to go for walks and spend time in the garden. These are things we naturally did before the lockdown, but now that our parents were making it compulsory, we teenagers wanted to rebel against these impositions. We had to get up each morning and complete an exercise routine that a global fitness guru, Joe Wicks, had put together. My ten-year-old brother, Flynn, and I totally lost interest after the first five days of the lockdown. Dad, however, continued to insist we do the routines. Freddie loved the exercise sessions in the morning. He took it upon himself to wake Flynn and me up for this! A lot of the morning routine was coordinated by dad because mum usually started working as early as 8 a.m. Dad made sure we exercised, got dressed, had our breakfast and got set up to complete our school tasks before he sat down to his work around 9.30 a.m. Mum and dad took turns throughout the day engaging Freddie as he was not able to work independently on his own like Flynn and I could.

Working on school tasks on the computer was just not the same as being in a classroom, but I was glad not to have to wear a uniform or have the teachers around. I loved that I could get through my schoolwork at my own pace, although you often had to wait for hours to get responses to queries sent to the teachers. Once I had done my schoolwork, I spent hours browsing the internet or playing computer games to pass the time. I did not enjoy the constant check-ins from my parents, and my friends were also experiencing the same thing. We all reminisced about the things we used to take for granted, like after-school activities, hanging out and meeting up at the local Costa café on weekend afternoons to chat and behave like adults. Instead, we spent more time online watching Netflix and uploading videos on TikTok. Snapchat also had its place. My friends and I often discussed the people we knew who we messaged but never heard back from.

Keeping safe and not being carriers of the virus became a social responsibility that we all took on. Those of us with grandparents talked about how we could only hold FaceTime calls with them. I missed the socialisation with people beyond my immediate family.

The end of the lockdown seemed more and more distant as it became obvious the number of cases and deaths were rising. Without a doubt, the world was fighting a war with an invisible enemy that it had no idea how to combat, and I was alive to witness this war. I would be part of the statistics quoted whenever this war was referred to in the future. If I survived to become an adult, I would be the one sharing the lockdown stories with generations who would only read about it in history books, as I had about the First and Second World Wars. The thought of it all only fed my curiosity and anxiety. There was always a question at the back of my mind. Will humanity ever get this virus under control?

Chapter 2:
Easter Holiday in Lockdown

How can I explain?
That while the sun shone on empty streets
And grasses grew tall in nearby parks
With flowers blooming with the start of spring
We were forced to stay safe indoors.

How can I explain?
That going out was now a danger
And a friend was to be treated like a stranger
That leaving the house was for set tasks
We were forced to stay safe indoors.

How can I explain?
That Easter will be a private affair
And loved ones can only be seen virtually
That touch from another could make me ill
As I was forced to stay safe indoors.

How can I explain?
That the world I took for granted
Was asking me to take a pause
To reflect on the damage done by humans
As I was forced to stay safe indoors.

'Favour, it is almost noon and you are still in bed. Get up! You are not going to sleep all through your Easter break!'

I woke up to my father's voice saying these words. I opened my eyes and glanced at him standing at my bedroom door. His presence lifted me out of my dream-like state. I rolled over in my double bed, still under my duvet, and muttered an acknowledgement of his words. After he left, I continued to lie in bed and stare at my white-painted ceiling. I could see the shadows my black-and-white lampshade cast against the wall spilling on to the hanging paintings, drawings and plaques. The sunlight was streaming around the sides of my still-lowered window blinds. My eyes travelled around the perimeter of my room as I tried to bring myself to be fully awake. The clothes I'd worn the day before were strewn on the floor. I smiled as I thought how lucky I was that dad had missed this. He always gave me a row for leaving my clothes and stuff all over the floor. I was now wide awake but still reluctant to get out of my warm bed. I rolled to the side and reached for a friendship pillow my best friend, Lucy, had given me for my twelfth birthday. Lucy has been my best friend since nursery school. We have a lot in common and share similar interests. She lives just three streets away from me and we have been walking to school together since primary 6. Our parents usually booked us into the same holiday camps and activities. I could trust her with any secret. We were in the same class and group in school, and since we lived so close, we were often together out of school too.

Today was 4 April 2020 and the start of the Easter holidays in Scotland. As I clutched the pillow, my thoughts continued to wander. Every Easter holiday, Lucy and I attended a week-long residential scripture union camp where we met kids like us from other parts of Scotland. The camp always involved a lot of outdoor activities and teachings on life skills. Thanks to the lockdown, the camp was cancelled. With no camp, I would probably wake up late each day with a plan to do very little. I was still struggling to accept that everything happening in the world was real. I fervently wished for it to be a temporary experience.

The weather forecast for the weekend was warm and humid with a lot of sunshine. I thought the weather was mocking us as we had nowhere to go and could not celebrate the warm spring weather as we typically would. A day like this would have meant a trip to the beach or a park for a picnic. My mum loved making us take advantage of the good weather as such days are golden in this part of the world. I wondered what limited family outdoor adventure was in store for us thanks to the lockdown! I recalled the news from the night before. Another 684 people had died in UK hospitals, and one of them was an NHS nurse. This brought the total number of UK coronavirus deaths to 3,605. The reporters said this was the highest daily death rate yet witnessed. The total world deaths due to coronavirus were now reported to be 58,773, with over one million people now known to be infected. The Secretary of State for Health and Social Care, Matt Hancock, had instructed people to continue to observe social distancing measures and encouraged frequent washing of hands. The prime minister emphasised that no one should be tempted to flout the rules during the warm weather weekend.

The first of the government's coronavirus field hospitals, dubbed Nightingale Hospitals, was opened in East London's ExCeL centre by Prince Charles via video link. I thought it was interesting that protocols to have a royal open such an establishment were still in place, even if it had to be done via video. The news on 25 March had reported that Prince Charles himself had tested positive for the virus after showing mild symptoms. The prince was recovering and was doing well, which was a great relief to me. I certainly did not want the nation to deal with any royal deaths in this pandemic! Even the Queen and Prince Philip were shielding – at Windsor Castle, having vacated Buckingham Palace. Each time I sat to watch the daily news, the scale of this deadly virus, with currently no cure, worsened my anxiety. I was hoping that a cure could be found to stop people from dying this way. I often wondered how I could help, but then I would quickly remind myself that I was helping by staying at home!

The noise of my brothers arguing downstairs jolted me back from my thoughts. I got up from my bed and picked up my strewn clothes from the floor in case dad came back to the room, then walked to the bathroom to get ready for the day. After about fifteen minutes in the bathroom, I returned to my bedroom and sat in front of the mirror on my dressing table to tidy up my hair. As I brushed and plaited my hair into two straight French braids, I looked at my reflection in the mirror and thought of how my life was wasting away with the lockdown. After what felt like an eternity gazing at myself, I got up to leave my room. As I stepped into the hallway, I was hit by the smell of warm pancakes *We must be having a family brunch*, I thought. My parents tend only to cook Saturday brunch during the holidays because it is impossible to accomplish during term time with my brothers' football training and matches, as this meant an early start for most Saturday mornings. I was lucky that whenever I had sporting activities on a Saturday, they were usually later in the afternoon.

On my way downstairs, I stopped by my parents' room to pick up my mobile phone. We had a rule in our house that no electronic gadgets (mobile phones, tablets, handheld game consoles) were allowed overnight in our rooms. All gadgets had to be handed in for recharging in my parents' room by 9 p.m. every evening. We were sure to receive a reminder if it was past nine and the gadgets were not plugged into their spots on my mum's dressing table. More importantly, they had to be switched off, as I for one have been guilty of receiving noisy alerts in the night that woke them up. As I picked up my phone, I saw two missed calls and three text messages from Peter. Now let me tell you a bit about Peter. Peter is one of my very good friends at school. He is very funny and smart. He is witty and clever with words and has a sound mind for science. We are often project and laboratory partners in school. He is a reliable friend and I can tell him anything. He was one of the few people from school that I had a daily catch-up with, and he always had some clever ways to share on how to pass the days in lockdown. We were in the same virtual group during last term's home-schooling and his presence in the virtual group often added a bit of colour and flavour to the otherwise dull classes. As I clicked on the texts, I wondered why Peter would have tried to contact me five times before noon on the first day of the Easter holidays. The words hit me like a tonne of bricks: *My grandfather died last night from coronavirus while in the hospital recovering from a fall.*

My head began to spin. Suddenly this virus was hitting closer to home. I sent him a text straight back: *Are you OK? Do you want to talk about it?*

Death is not something I have much experience of dealing with, and I was unsure how best to support Peter. I decided the best thing to do was talk to my mum about it. I was sure she would know what to do. There were two other texts from Lucy and Kimberly asking what I was planning for the day.

As I stepped out of my parents' room, mum called out, 'Favour! Where are you?' I responded, 'Coming, mum,' and made my way quickly down the stairs. As I walked into the kitchen, I saw that she was flipping the last batch of pancakes and dad was transferring the bacon from the grill pan onto a plate. Mum looked up. 'Ah, there you are, Favour. Lay the table, will you?' I nodded and smiled at her and dad. 'Sure,' I said. The thought of having fluffy pancakes with grilled bacon and syrup lifted my mood. I still believe that mum makes the best pancakes in the world. She is great at paying attention to detail whenever she is cooking. I grabbed the plates from the cupboard then stopped. 'I've had some bad news from Peter,' I said. 'He's just lost his grandfather to Covid-19.' Mum placed the last batch of pancakes with the others, switched off the gas cooker and pulled me close. I put the plates down on the kitchen counter, and as I submitted to her warm embrace tears started pricking the backs of my eyelids. At this stage, I was not sure if the tears were falling because of my closeness to Peter or because of my overall frustration with the impact the virus was having on my life. One thing was clear, though, the hug made me feel better. Mum knew what good friends Peter and I were and understood how I felt. After a moment or so in her embrace, I pulled away and picked up the plates to resume the task of setting the dining table. As I was walking out of the kitchen, mum said, 'Peter must be devastated. Have you spoken to him yet?'

'I sent him a text asking if he was OK and if he wanted to talk about it,' I replied.

'That is very thoughtful.' She smiled. 'Give him space to get back to you in his own time.'

'I wish I could be of help,' I said.

Mum thought for a second. 'Why not design a virtual sympathy card and send it to him?' she suggested. 'That will show him that you are thinking about him as a good friend should.'

'That is a great idea. Thanks, mum!' I said as I left the room, happy to have a plan to reach out to Peter in a way that would have some meaning. I put the plates on the dining room table and returned to the kitchen to grab the cutlery. Flynn joined me to set the table. He picked up the drinking glasses and my parents followed us carrying the food. After a final trip to the kitchen to get syrup, lemon juice, butter and jam, the table was set for brunch.

We all sat down, and dad said grace. We passed the bowls and plates across the table and helped ourselves. I heaped butter and syrup on the two pancakes on my plate and cut the three strips of bacon up, concentrating on getting the set-up of the food on my plate just right. As I took the first forkful, mum asked us how it felt to finally be on Easter break and away from home-schooling. Flynn and I responded with whoops of delight. Even Freddie joined in to express his happiness. As we ate, we chatted about the plans for the day. Dad said we would be going for a family bike ride later in the afternoon since it was turning out to be a very warm day. As they always did, dad complimented mum on the food, saying how wonderful the pancakes were, and mum thanked him for his help in the kitchen. This way they have, of displaying their affection, never gets old with me and I would usually tease them about it with a comment. However today, my thoughts were on the design of the virtual card I was going to make for Peter.

We finished the meal and Flynn and I cleared the table, as was our expected routine after every meal. Mum assigned me to wash the dishes while Flynn was instructed to clean the table and put the placemats and coasters away. Tidying up after a meal was important to mum and this emphasis had been heightened by my parents since the lockdown. Once the kitchen was all tidied up with plates, cutlery and pans put away in the cupboards and drawers, I went back to my room. I passed mum, who was now working away on a corner of the dining table she had set up as her office space. She seemed to be working longer hours, and I know this was probably one of the effects of the lockdown. I spotted out of the corner of my eye that Flynn and Freddie had gone into the garden to play a game of football with dad. I stopped to pick up my laptop in my parents' room and went back to my room to work. I set the laptop on the desk in the corner of my room. This same desk had served as my virtual classroom for the past two weeks. My collection of novels by David Walliams and Jacqueline Wilson still sat in an orderly stack on the left-hand side of the desk. I felt I had outgrown the books but having them on the desk was a reminder of a part of my childhood that I was not ready to let go. Up until recently, I was a fan of David Walliams and possessed all the books he had ever written. Now my reading list included classics written by authors like Robert Louis Stevenson. I love to read and there is never a time that I do not have a book to hand. My favourite time of the day for reading is at night when everyone has gone to bed. Curling up under my duvet and escaping into the worlds created by the authors is a daily treat I would not miss.

To the right of the desk was a lava lamp I was given for my ninth birthday. I switched on the laptop and started the drawing app. At that very moment, my phone pinged with a text alert. It was from Peter. He acknowledged my text with the response, *I am OK. Not in the mood to talk right now but thanks for the offer.* I felt the message reflected the pain that Peter must be going through. I began the task of creating the card. I settled for a butterfly flying away from a green meadow. Drawing and painting have been a passion of mine, and my bedroom wall was a testament to my past work, including self-portraits both in paint and pencil, as well as some still life pieces. Art is one of my favourite subjects, and drawing comes naturally to me with little effort. As I settled down to design Peter's card, I made a mental note to add drawing and painting to the list of activities to keep me busy for the lockdown. I spent the next forty minutes designing the card, and once it was complete, I sent it to Peter.

At 3 p.m., dad hollered to us kids to get ready to cycle out to a nearby village, about five miles away. Cycling was one of the forms of exercise that my family had added to the list of traditions we were developing during the lockdown. We tried not to cycle too far because of Freddie still being quite small. Mum packed bottles of water and snacks for the trip. We set out and made a stop at a park that is halfway to the village. We soaked up some sunshine, enjoying the warm weather. Even though I did not always enjoy being dragged out on these family daily exercises, I knew that the fresh air was for my good, but my teenage mind was not willing to openly admit this to my parents. After thirty minutes, we continued our trip until we reached the village. As expected, it was all very quiet, just a few people out walking, some with their dogs. We stopped for a short rest then cycled straight back home. By the time we got back, I felt refreshed and energised.

It was now nearly 5 p.m. and mum thought it would be a great idea to have homemade pizza with everyone making their own. She had made the dough and left it to prove before we set out, and it was now ready. Creative meals, like homemade pizza, were another thing added to our list of family traditions, and they were welcomed by everyone because it still felt like an individual activity and we could all make ours just how we liked it. Mum divided up the dough and everyone got a corner of the kitchen table to prepare their pizza base. With our individual baking trays, we made our pizzas and put generous toppings of sauce, ham, meatballs, pepperoni and cheese. I had to admit that making homemade pizza was a healthier alternative to ordering takeaway pizza, though I still looked forward to when the lockdown was over, as I would still love a few slices of Domino's pizza!

Once the pizzas were baked, we sat down to eat. Mealtimes provided a focus for the day, but there were times when all that cooking took its toll. I seemed to spend a considerable amount of time in the kitchen either helping to prepare main meals or simply looking for snacks to kill the boredom. The previous weekend, we had made chocolate chip cookies and blondie brownies. Mum was using the baking to keep us occupied and stock the house with goodies. I love baking, but when my brothers are involved, the fun is quickly eroded and one of my parents needs to be on standby to act as a referee!

Once the meal was finished, we watched the news and learnt that another 760 people had died in the UK. I couldn't help but think that Peter's grandad was one of the 760. I checked my email, but still no response from Peter.

I decided to retreat to my room to FaceTime Lucy and my other friends and catch up on their day. Peter did not join the call, but he had sent us all a text about his grandad's passing. We were all sorry to know that our friend was in a sad place. Josh shared how he had gone fishing with Peter and his grandad last summer, and from what he knew they were very close. Kimberly's parents are both doctors who work with the NHS. Her dad is a cardiologist while her mum is a paediatrician. She shared how concerned her parents were about the whole situation. Lucy was sad that the lockdown prevented us from paying Peter a visit. We continued to chat for another hour before ending the call. Seeing as it was just 9 p.m., I decided to play Roblox. It's one of my favourite online games, and I played a lot more of it during the lockdown. I think it was the ability to design game characters that made me love this game. I played Roblox every day of lockdown and improved my gaming skills in the process. I sometimes also play Fortnite, but Roblox is still my favourite. Just before bedtime, I got a text from Peter thanking me for the card and how touched he was by it. I was so glad that he liked it.

The rest of the Easter holiday dragged on, and for most of it, all I could think about was how bored I was. Just before Easter, we began to clap every Thursday for the NHS front-line staff, the idea being it was a way for everyone to show an appreciation for the sacrifices they were making for all of us. This weekly tradition added another flavour to the lockdown. My father rounded us up for this session each week. Freddie looked forward to the session the most. You could see by the way he clapped the hardest with so much enthusiasm how his young mind interpreted this as part of the things we had to do to control the spread of the virus. Seeing everyone come out of their houses and clap in unison was a reminder of the war that we were fighting, and that the NHS staff were the ones waging the war our behalf from the front line. Kimberly shared with us how her parents felt humbled by this gesture of gratitude from the public. This made me determined not to break the lockdown rules, even though I was tempted on many occasions. The fact that some of the NHS staff were dying from the virus made the whole situation so sad, and I did not want to be responsible for putting the lives of Kimberly's parents at risk. The NHS front-line staff were like soldiers falling to the enemy's bullet in battle with little to defend themselves. As a family, we made donations to charities that supported obtaining adequate PPE for NHS staff. We also supported the ninety-nine-year-old war veteran Captain Tom Moore, who completed 100 laps in his garden to raise money for NHS charities. In the end, Captain Moore raised an impressive thirty-three million pounds!

As the Easter weekend approached, the warmer weather made it difficult to stay indoors. We kept up with our daily walking or cycling. On 5 April the UK prime minister, Boris Johnson, was admitted to the hospital with Covid-19 symptoms. Hearing the news that evening gripped me with a renewed fear of the virus. This disease did not discriminate! If the prime minister could contract it, then surely nobody was safe! My family prayed for the recovery of the prime minister. My mind was beginning to battle with itself. What was the world going to do about this invisible deadly enemy? I decided to carry out some research online on how I could treat myself if I contracted the disease. As you can imagine, the web was filled with a lot of information and claims that drugs like chloroquine (an antimalarial drug) could cure it! No doubt our gullibility was being exploited and it did not help that some world leaders were encouraging this. In my opinion, the world leaders supporting this propaganda were trying to demonstrate, at all cost, that they had everything under control!

The Thursday before Easter, I went out shopping with dad. This was my first shopping experience since lockdown. When we arrived at the shop, the long queue of people was very daunting. The experience felt like a scene out of the movie. Everyone had a face mask on. It was at this moment the term 'the new normal' became real to me. Wearing of facemasks when you went out had become as normal as putting on your coat. I was uncomfortable wearing a face mask as I struggled to breathe throughout the shopping trip. I was glad that we were only in the shop to get a few items. As soon as we stepped outside, I took off my face mask to fill my lungs with fresh air. This is the fresh air that up until that moment, I had never thought much about. I was thankful for the gift of being able to breathe freely.

On Easter Sunday, my parents did their best to cheer us up. We were all getting bothered and edgy being in the house all the time. After we had each polished off a bacon roll and a cup of hot chocolate, they played a game of football with us. As mum held her own during the game, I was reminded that she had played football back in her school days. The rest of my family are keen football fans, but I'm not a fan of playing garden football or even football as a spectator sport. However, my parents made it clear that I had no choice but to join in, and it turned out to be much fun and a great way to start the Easter Sunday.

After we had finished the game, it was time for our traditional Easter Sunday roast lunch with all the trimmings. Mum had got up early to prepare a wonderful meal. She put in the same effort as she always did. This year, we were having duck, and it was roasting nicely while we were out in the garden playing football. The only thing missing was that we had no guests to share it with. My parents love entertaining friends, and I think it must have been hard on them to just celebrate all by ourselves. This was another impact that the virus had on our lives.

Mum made up for the lack of contact with friends by volunteering in the community, picking up prescriptions and doing essential shopping for those who had to stay isolated or shielded from the virus. Every other day, I would see her happily going out to help others. Each time she returned from one of these errands she always quoted the saying that we are *blessed to be a blessing*. I truly admire this selfless act of love that my mum so happily gave to others. As a family, we reached out to those who were in need and helped the best we could. Dad and I joined in my school's virtual race challenge to raise money for charity. Flynn's football club joined in the community anchor project to deliver food parcels every weekend.

Flynn and I helped to set the table and we sat down to have our meal. We talked a lot about how different it was celebrating Easter this year and what we would do for the rest of the day. After the wonderful roast lunch, our parents told us that there was an Easter egg hunt in the garden for us kids. Unknown to us, dad had spent all morning hiding the eggs as mum prepared the Easter meal. I could not believe how much this simple game got me so upbeat. I was running around the garden like a little girl in search of the hidden chocolate eggs. I would normally think that I was too old for an Easter egg hunt, but the lockdown broke down my barriers, and I had so much fun. After twenty minutes, I had a basket full of Easter eggs to feast on over the next few days! I posted so many pictures on TikTok and Instagram so that my followers could share in my fun. Flynn found the most hidden eggs and won the golden rabbit prize. This turned out to be the best day of the Easter holidays.

My friends and I were becoming increasingly apprehensive during the last week of the Easter holidays. We were hoping that we would get to go back to school in some sort of fashion. But the weekly updates by the first minister of Scotland on 8 April, dashed this hope when she announced that schools would not be reopening for the summer term but rather, we were to continue virtual learning. I broke into tears after the announcement. It seemed as if there was no end to the lockdown in sight. At this point, my need for physical contact with my friends was so acute that I lost all interest in everything. I became lethargic and uninterested in the family walks and cycling. It became a chore to spend time with my family. I just wanted to pass the days in my room playing Roblox or drawing. Even the new family traditions of baking and Saturday brunch had lost their appeal. I was just angry, and I wanted answers. The more I drew or painted, the more I produced drawings that were showing how I felt inside. One of my drawings was a picture of a girl in chains reaching out for freedom. I also drew a picture of a girl holding her head in both hands.

The universe was at a standstill, and no one was sure what to do to get it moving again. I wanted to understand how a virus from faraway China, could shut down the whole world this way. I wanted someone to reassure me that my family and friends were safe. At this point, I knew of four people who had died of the virus. Apart from Peter's grandfather, there were three of dad's friends and associates down in London. The prime minister was still recovering from the virus. Things didn't feel safe, yet I craved my friends' company so much, and our daily chats were dominated by our frustrations with the lockdown. We were tired. Peter was withdrawn after his grandfather's death. He was slow responding to messages and declined to join our daily FaceTime call; not that I blame him. He had shared with me that following the government's restrictions on funeral attendance, very few people had come to his grandfather's funeral and this had made him very sad. His grandad, his mum's dad, had worked for many years offshore in the oil and gas industry and had made a lot of friends along the way. The restrictions meant that none of his good friends could come and say goodbye, which made Peter's mum very upset about the whole situation. You could tell that going through the whole funeral had been very tough on Peter and his family. Peter's slow responses to my texts demonstrated to me that he was struggling with this blow life had dealt him, and I kept thinking about how I couldn't be there for him, given his friends were not physically able to support him. My mum advised me to check on him maybe twice a week and just give him space until he was ready. But it all made me feel helpless.

My parents must have sensed the effect of not going back to school was having on me. They started spending one-to-one time with me just to chat. I would either vent my frustrations or tell them everything was fine so that I could be left alone. My parents then took the step of signing me up to attend some virtual community programmes arranged by the local church. This proved to be a much-needed respite from the dark world I found myself in. The group's activities gave me something new to do, and we talked about the real challenges teenagers like me were facing during the lockdown, and then sometimes we just played games and listened to music. The therapy I received from this virtual engagement was huge. The group helped me to mentally prepare for the summer term, and I gradually found my positivity again.

Chapter 3:
Summer Term in Lockdown

Working from home and virtual learning
Mobile banking and online shopping
Cars parked in driveways while people walk
Staying two metres apart to greet and talk
This is the new normal.

Home baking and garden barbecues
Virtual consultations with GPs and doctors on Zoom
Watching TV to pass the time
Tuning in to the six o'clock news
This is the new normal.

Restaurants and pubs are shut
High street shops are going bust
Government trying to maintain control
While the virus claims the sick and the old
This is the new normal.

Household bubbles are created
NHS heroes are appreciated
Travel distances are regulated
Virtual check-ins from family and friends
This is the new normal.

Wash your hands and wear a face mask
Keep meetings virtual or outdoors
Maintain a daily exercise to keep fit and well
If you must touch anything use a hand gel
This is the new normal.

So far, this sounds like a completely dark story with no fun or joy. Well, to be honest, that is what it felt like at the time. It was 20 April, and the summer term had begun. The news from the previous day reported that the total number of UK deaths were now at 16,509. The British Broadcasting Corporation (BBC) highlighted that there were 8,000 more deaths than normal during a similar time in previous years. Hospital leaders continued to attack the government for lack of Personal Protective Equipment (PPE). The global cases of the virus had now passed 2.4 million. The numbers just seemed to keep rising.

The perfect thoughts in my head about learning from home, not having to wear school uniform, fewer classes, no teachers watching over you in person, had all lost their appeal. The last two weeks of the spring term had been a breeze, and at the time, I'd thought home-schooling was quite fun. This time around, the weeks of completing schoolwork online was nowhere as easy as I thought it would be, and this caught me off guard. I had completely disregarded the fact that my family being around was a distraction.

We used Microsoft Teams and OneNote for our virtual classes. The teachers loaded our daily tasks before the start of the school day, and I tried to complete most of them on time. I continued to work on my lessons from the desk set up in my room. On most days, my bedroom window reflected the bright clear skies and the green garden of our home. The thought of being outside with my friends often filled my mind as I worked through the tasks. I would frequently try and sneak a chat with them. Lucy and Kimberly were as distracted as I was, and it was great that we had Josh and Peter as friends because they both created physical exercise routines for us as a group. We often joked about not getting flabby! I was very relieved to find that, by the start of the summer term, Peter had recovered from the loss of his grandad and was back to his normal witty self.

My parents constantly came into my room to check that I was working on my school tasks as expected. I found this distracting as I was trying to concentrate. Teamwork was also a challenge to complete as some students in the class just worked at their own pace and delayed submitting their required contributions for group assignments. This frustrated me, and the lower grades that were often awarded consequently added to my frustration. It was obvious that learning from home was not for me.

Sometimes, Freddie would wander into my room asking me to keep him company or play a game with him outside in the garden, and I tried my best to balance it all. It is hard to describe how my feelings fluctuated almost every day. I went from confused, shocked and scared to irritable and tearful. I swung from one emotional level to another with no warning. I felt so unfortunate to be confined to within the walls of my home with so many rules! One thing a kid like me does not enjoy is having to obey too many rules. But as you can imagine, that is exactly what I had to put up with. I hated being told what to do and how to live my life by people who had no idea what it was like for teenagers like me.

Lunch break during the school term had to be fitted into my parents' work schedule. Mum and dad tried to keep it simple so that it did not take a lot of time to prepare. I had to help on most days, and this was another source of distraction. I missed going to the nearby shops during the school lunch break to buy my lunch and eat whatever I wanted while hanging out with my friends. Now lunchtime was another family time with questions being asked that I frankly did not want to answer. Being at home all together also meant increased household chores that had to be completed. I often fell out with Flynn because he would not do his bit, such as cleaning the dining table and sweeping the kitchen floor after each meal. Freddie would make a mess, like spilling water or juice, and this had to be cleaned up. I wanted freedom and a break from it all, but that felt like a reality that would never come. I started opting to eat my lunch later by working longer on my school tasks in the mornings. I found this a very useful tactic that kept me away from the family lunch hour.

The longer daylight hours meant we could take family walks in the lengthening evenings. I enjoyed watching the landscape change – the sights, sounds and smells, as the season progressed. We would get a whiff of manure and spot the farmers working away in their tractors, see the nearby farmlands first ploughed then planted, and watch the herds of cows or flocks of sheep grazing nearby. The wildflowers, well-trimmed hedges and lawns with bushes budding with flowers created a beautiful backdrop. We often met a people we knew during these family walks, either working away in their front gardens or going for walks themselves, but we never stopped to chat. We had to wave a greeting while maintaining a two-metre gap between us.

The good weather must have been working on my mood because I suddenly started enjoying the family evening walks again. Before the virus, I was at school for long hours, my parents worked for even longer and there were different school finishing times for my brothers and me. After our dinner, dad would have several online meetings with people from all over the world and mum would be working again. Fitting in times for family games or walks was almost impossible. The lockdown helped my parents to find the time to spend with us. Our relationship as a family was getting better, and the new traditions of baking, making homemade pizza and Saturday pancake brunch continued. I was also enjoying the virtual youth group. Flynn began to join me on some occasions, and surprisingly, this wasn't so bad. There were conferences set up that Flynn and I attended online with guest speakers from all over the county. It brought another dimension to the virtual group. Often the speakers were young adults, and this made them relatable. They spoke about their struggles with the lockdown and life in general, and I enjoyed listening to them as they shared their experiences. It was reassuring not to feel alone in my struggles.

My parents tried to take us out in turn for the weekly food shopping just to create some variety in our restricted lives and spend one-to-one time with us. I loved these moments because I could influence the shopping list, and I often got to pick one item of my choice, but I still hated the experience of wearing a face mask as we shopped. I was always glad to get outside into the fresh air. The queues into the shops were improving and the two-metre distancing had been marked on all shop floors. Trolleys and baskets had to be self-sanitised and the use of hand gels with the wearing of face masks was encouraged. I always tried to check what was different from my last shopping experience. The shelves were better stocked each time, and I thought this was good. It also meant that the NHS staff were probably getting enough supplies during their allocated shopping hours. Finally, the hoarding frenzy was easing off.

Then, at last, the number of deaths from the virus began to drop after the largest death count of 20 April. It seemed as if the restrictions and lockdown were finally paying off. The prime minister had fully recovered and was back at work. He kept reassuring the nation that once the rate of spread of the virus i.e. Reproduction (R) number, fell below one, the lockdown would be eased. Seeing the death rates drop was very encouraging. We did not have to wait for too long.

On 29 May, the government put in new rules, easing the lockdown. We were now allowed to meet up with another household in outdoor spaces, but not exceeding a total number of eight. When we met people from other households, we had to maintain the two-metre social distancing. We could travel more than five miles out of our homes in cars. Indoor gatherings were still banned, but that was OK. The first thing I did was arrange to meet with my friends. We could go to parks and shops, just not into each other's homes. That evening, during our FaceTime call, my friends and I agreed to meet the following Saturday at 3 p.m. for a picnic in a nearby park. We planned to bring our own food and go for a walk afterwards. I welcomed this development with a lot of excitement, and I felt so much better. I offered to do more around the house without complaining. My parents were delighted that I was chirpier and brighter. I planned carefully for the Saturday picnic with my four friends.

Saturday came and by 2.30 p.m., I'd packed my brown leather backpack with a bacon and cheese sandwich, a slice of homemade Victoria sponge, a red apple, a packet of custard cream biscuits and two bottles of water. I checked that I had hand sanitiser, a picnic blanket and a face mask in my bag before heading out. My parents warned me not to make any physical contact and to try and maintain the social distance rule while hanging out with my friends. I felt a sense of responsibility with this trust, and I was determined not to let my parents down. When I arrived at the park at 2.55 p.m., Josh, Peter and Kimberly were already there. We exchanged greetings and chatted away until Lucy joined us two minutes later. We sat in a very wide circle that allowed us to maintain the social distancing rules and ate our food while we chatted. We talked so much you wouldn't believe we had daily FaceTime chats with each other. It was good to finally see Peter in person. He seemed to have matured during the lockdown and was taller than I last remembered. Peter got us to play a game of truth or dare. It was so much fun that not having physical contact did not matter. We talked about the fifth year and sixth year students who would not take exams, but have their results assessed from their performance history in school. We were glad not to be in their shoes!

We were enjoying each other's company so much that we lost track of time and missed our planned walk. By 6 p.m., we packed up, said our goodbyes and headed home. I was so happy to have spent the time with my friends without breaking the social distancing rules. I felt this was an example of how we teenagers could be trusted.

When I got home, Freddie met me by the door and said, 'Favour, you need to wash your hands because I don't want you to bring the germs into the house!' He ushered me to the bathroom to wash my hands and I sang the happy birthday song with him watching. Once this was completed, he left me in peace. I went to the kitchen to empty my backpack. Mum had started dinner and I recounted all that had transpired with my friends. She smiled and said, 'I can see that meeting up with your friends has returned the twinkle in your eyes.' I laughed so hard at this. Then dad joined us in the kitchen. He was pleased to know that I'd had fun. That evening, Mum made burgers, sweetcorn and chips for dinner. As we ate, I reflected about the whole experience of the lockdown to date. I thought about how far we had come and the renewed possibilities of seeing my friends.

After dinner, it began to rain so we were unable to go out for a walk. We watched a movie on Netflix together as a family, and dad made us all popcorn. My mood was so positive that even Flynn noticed it. While I'd gone for a picnic with my friends, Flynn had been cycling with his friend, Robbie. It was such a great day to feel free again. That night, I went to bed happy with hope.

My mum's birthday is on 28 June, and each year dad always does his best to make her feel special. He was determined that this year would not be any different, even with the lockdown. Since we could not go out for a meal, dad engaged Flynn and me to make the day memorable. We baked and decorated a cake the day before while Mum stayed away from the kitchen. Dad also got a Costco cake just in case the cake we made went horribly wrong. However, ours turned out very well, and we had a lot of cake to eat! This year, Mum's birthday fell on a Sunday and dad made the Sunday roast for lunch. We helped in the kitchen while Mum read a book and made FaceTime calls to family and friends in the bedroom. We called her downstairs at noon, and she was speechless when she saw all the effort we had made. When she found her words, she said, 'My darlings, this is beautiful. Thank you so much. My day is perfect.' We sat down to eat and she complimented us on how tasty everything was and how she preferred the homemade cake to the Costco cake. This was the only family birthday we celebrated during the full lockdown, and I think Mum will forever remember it!

On 3 July, the last day of the summer term finally came. We had been in lockdown for 103 days. It was great to come to the end of the school term and I was happy to have survived it all. I knew that my academic performance had not been the best, but I tried not to think about it.

Since the picnic, my friends and I had met up a couple more times, and life felt so much better with the easing of the lockdown. The Scottish government announced that the rules were changing further the day before the end of term with phased changes over two weeks. Wearing face masks would be compulsory in shops but not for under-11-year-olds. Since I had always worn a face mask going into the shops, the change made little difference to me. Restaurants and hotels could open with strict guidelines, and contact sports for children and young people were started up again.

Freddie was graduating from nursery school, but unfortunately, he would not get to see any of his friends, or the nursery staff, again before starting primary school. I felt so sad for him that he would not have a proper graduation ceremony like Flynn and I had when we left nursery school. We made up for it by holding a ceremony for him at home. I don't think Freddie knew the difference as he just loved the attention he was getting and dressing up in his homemade graduation gown, which I had helped to make following some instructions and a YouTube video sent by the nursery. He used my mum's old graduation cap for full effect and sent two pictures to the nursery for their records.

As the summer holiday was about to begin, it seemed as if life was finally getting back to normal. I went hillwalking with my friends to celebrate the end of the term. It was a great experience, though I found it hard at the start of the walk because of the weeks of not playing any form of sport. By the time we got midway, my muscles had loosened up and I made it to the top. Kimberly struggled, though, and we all had to support her to get to the top. We teased Kimberly because of the five of us, she had been the least active, but this was no fault of her own. As Kimberly's parents were doctors, they were hardly at home and Kimberly had been attending the government schools set up for front-line workers. She had been spending a lot of time on her own most evenings. During our daily calls, she often shared her concern for her parents' safety. She went through a lot of scary moments when it was reported that NHS staff were contracting the virus because of the lack of PPE, and some of them were dying from it. However, with the infection rate dropping, the impact on the NHS seemed to be eased. We made it to the top and Kimberly recovered so well that she got back down on her own. We were so proud of her.

Afterwards, we went for lunch at the local McDonald's. Well, we all got a takeaway and ate the food in the park. We were still unsure about sitting inside a restaurant and preferred to eat in the safety of the outside fresh air. This was one of the scars that the virus had left us with. We talked about our plans for summer, and it was obvious that we were all going for some form of summer break with our families. We promised to keep in touch and parted ways. This was a great start to the summer holiday, and I was looking forward to having a relatively normal one.

Chapter 4:
Summer Holiday in Lockdown

The street silence is gripping
The news is disturbing
People are restless with being indoors
Yet the sun shines hot and bright
As the lockdown goes on.

The rules are eased for travel and meetings
But with guidelines and warnings
Groups of eight can meet for fun
If they stay outdoors in the sun
As the lockdown goes on.

Fields are ploughed for the next harvest
Animals grazing with no bother nearby
Joggers and cyclists dominate the roads
Families trying to stay positive and cope
As the lockdown goes on.

We should be away on summer vacation
With beaches and endless rays of sunshine
Instead, the airports are eerily quiet
With everyone opting for a staycation
As the lockdown goes on.

This was the summer we will never forget
With changes to plans made months ahead
We will never forget the year in our lives
That gave a new meaning to human existence
As the lockdown went on.

Now, you may be wondering, what my plans were for the long summer holidays. Well, to be honest, I didn't have any plans. Maybe a bit of baking, binge-watching Netflix, YouTube, playing more Roblox and Fortnite, but nothing meaningful or even interesting. Every day was going to be the same as any other normal lazy day. Week after week of sleeping until noon, having a shower for an hour, then eating my 'breakfast' while lunch was already being prepared. Yes, that was the life I had planned for summer, which fitted the template of most teenagers like me.

This summer was so much hotter than I'd expected, and that caused me many long and sleepless nights. My parents stocked up on ice cream and ice lollies to cool us down during the day. I must have eaten a tonne of them during the summer! My parents took two weeks off to spend some time with us and get a break themselves from the long hours of work. Dad's birthday was in the first week of the summer holidays. There are only twelve days between mum's and dad's birthdays so every year, we get two weeks of celebrating. Since we'd had cake just twelve days ago, Mum decided to make a giant cookie cake for dad. It was spectacular! Mum is a great baker, and she told us she had been baking since she was ten! My brothers and I all learnt to bake from her, and we used the lockdown to learn new baking skills and recipes. Freddie baked a lot with mum during this period. Flynn and I are capable of baking unsupervised, and we often made a quick batch of chocolate chip cookies to satisfy our sweet tooth and fill the boredom. I also tried recipes like blondie brownies, lemon tart and even cheesecake. So yes, we baked a lot during the lockdown! Flour, eggs, butter, sugar and chocolate were always on the shopping list.

Mum made a haggis meal to celebrate dad's birthday this year. Haggis is a traditional Scottish dish usually eaten to celebrate Burns Night on 25 January – commemorating the birth of Scottish poet Robert (Rabbie) Burns. The good thing is that you can get haggis all year round, and we all love it! It was also a welcome change to our usual meals. The effort touched dad; it was a nice way to start the family holiday.

The following day, we set off for a week in Perth. Usually, we went abroad for at least a week or two of the summer holidays, but the virus made the idea of going abroad unsafe, so my parents planned instead for us to have a lovely staycation in the Tayside area of Scotland. Also, we didn't want to drive too far as Freddie and I usually get car sick on long journeys. They rented an apartment in Perth in the heart of the city. The idea was to spend each day doing something fun. Dad planned to get some relaxing alone time to play golf in between the family activities. Dad loves playing golf; it's his second favourite sport after football.

The apartment we rented was a three-bedroomed flat overlooking the River Tay. I got a room to myself while my brothers had to share. The decor and furnishings were modern. The building was three storeys high and our flat was on the second floor. It felt like living in a penthouse. It was great that the streets were still relatively quiet from the lockdown. We ate out most of the time or ordered takeaways.

The first day was spent visiting Blair Drummond Safari and Adventure Park. I loved that we had to book allocated times for our visit as it meant the park was not too busy and we could see all the available attractions. I was impressed by the measures that had been put in place, like one-way systems for crowd control, hand sanitisers at every attraction and hand-washing stations as you came out of the pet farm. As a result of the government rules on indoor activities and social distancing measures, the sea lion show and the face painting service were not available. However, there was still a lot to see. We spent five hours in the park, and it was the first time since the lockdown that I had been away from my gadgets for that long of my own free will! Before we visited, I had watched a viral video online about a family that had an interesting experience when they did the safari drive thru. A monkey had climbed on top of their car and pooped on the panoramic roof; the dad was furious. Another family had shared online how a monkey had snapped off the car's rear windscreen wiper. As we drove into the safari park, I wondered what experience was lurking around the corner for us.

We started by visiting the sea lions, penguins and pet farms with the alpacas, ponies, guinea pigs and rabbits. Freddie was very excited and animated throughout our visit to the pet farm. We then saw the meerkats, lemurs and otters and I was very impressed at the size of the tiger. Freddie wanted to go on the rides, while Flynn and I were indifferent because the rides we would have loved to go on, like the bungee trampolines, astroglide and flying fox, were closed because of the virus. In the end, Mum bought tickets for the dodgems. Then, because he couldn't go on his own, I was nominated to join Freddie on the spinning teacup ride, much to my displeasure!

After the rides, we were hungry. Mum had packed a picnic as she was unsure what food would be available in the park. We headed back to the car and got out the picnic basket, which was filled with everything we liked, from bacon sandwiches and crisps to cookies, fruit and drinks. We used one of the benches in the car park and were halfway through our feast when a light shower came out of nowhere! We hurriedly packed up, and by the time we'd put everything back in the car, the shower stopped and the sun began to shine again, much to our delight! I thought the weather was being cheeky!

After lunch, we visited the dinosaur park and saw some families cooking barbecues in the custom barbecue pits. I was amused at the thought of holding a barbecue in a safari park with all types of animals surrounding you! I was sure that if the animals could speak, they would express their displeasure!

When we got back to our car to move on to the next activity, there was a large, beautiful peacock blocking the rear door of the car. As I approached, it opened its plume of tail feathers and started walking towards me. I was terrified and panicked, as I thought it was going to attack us. Dad said we should use the opportunity to walk over and see the elephants and ostrich, and hopefully, when we got back, it would be gone. The peacock occupied my mind all through the visit to the elephant and ostrich enclosure. I only relaxed when Mum started taking pictures. Sure enough, by the time we got back to the car, the peacock had moved on. This was the first unusual experience of the day.

We next headed to the pedal boats and cruised around the lake. I sat in the front and pedalled the boat with dad with Freddie in between us, while Flynn and Mum sat at the back. It was nice to be moving around the water, and by now the peacock experience was behind me. Thanks to Freddie, we pedalled for much longer, but I was getting tired and wanted us to go and do something else. The promise of ice cream later finally got Freddie to agree to us returning to the waterside. We got off the boat, climbed straight into the car and headed to the Drive-Thru Safari. You had to stay in the car and keep your windows up. I shared the story with my family about the monkey that pooped on top of the car. Freddie did not like that idea at all and hoped it would not happen to us. As we approached the entrance of the drive, we saw a magnificent elephant. We took pictures, and when we entered the drive-thru the first animals we saw were the rhinos and camels. I was in awe of how the animals had adapted to living in a colder climate like Scotland's. We then continued into the enclosure holding the pride of lions. As we drove through, one of the lions came close to the car. Dad stopped and I was gripped with fear! Mum kept reassuring us to just be calm and take pictures. It took me a few seconds to recover as I thought it might jump on the car, but after gazing at us, it just walked to the other side of the road. This was my second unusual encounter of the day! We moved on until we came out into the enclosure with the monkeys. Luckily, they just played away and were not interested in climbing our car. Next were the antelopes. They looked so elegant and graceful.

We left the Drive-Thru Safari and went back to the car park so that we could visit the birds of prey and attend the final bird of prey show for the day. We saw various species of owls, a hawk, vultures, falcons and a kite. My favourite was the barn owl because of how mystic it looked. We headed for the show and sat down observing the two-metre rule. Flynn and I sat far away from our parents just to get some freedom to chat and watch the show without being under their watchful eyes. The show began and the Harris hawk was the first bird brought out for display. As the presenter released the bird, they kept telling us to duck our heads if the bird flew towards us. At the third release of the hawk, I decided not to duck my head, and suddenly the hawk was headed towards me at great speed, filling me with fright. It was an inch from my head before it changed direction and flew elsewhere. My parents had not seen it, and I kept still for the rest of the show. Only Flynn knew what happened and I swore him into silence. The second bird was a great grey owl, and unlike the hawk, it was calmer in its flying and approach. The presenter shared a lot about both birds, but my fear from the hawk shut me down for the rest of the bird show.

After the falconry, it was time to leave and head back to Perth. Mum bought the promised ice cream and we got into the car. I was quiet all through the drive, and I heard mum tell dad that I must be hungry. Usually, I get quiet and withdrawn when I am hungry, but this time, it was because I was still recovering from the hawk flying very close to my face! I wanted to chat with my friends on the phone, but my battery had died, and I could not find my charger in my bag. Freddie kept trying to engage with me, but I just wanted him to leave me alone! Mum sensed this and started playing a game of I spy with Freddie instead. Flynn kept glancing my way but said nothing and instead joined in the game of I spy with mum and Freddie. After an hour of driving, we got back to the apartment. We rested for a bit and then went down to a nearby restaurant for dinner. I was quiet all through the meal and just wanted to get to bed. When we got back, I plugged in my phone to charge, but my friends were not online. I decided to play Roblox on my phone and when it was 9 p.m., we all went to bed.

I felt much better when I woke up and was able to put the events of the previous day behind me. After a late breakfast, we set out to St

Andrews to spend the day at the beach while dad played golf. St Andrews is known for its majestic golf courses. It also has a beautiful seaside which is famous for campers. Mum dropped dad off at the golf links and we headed to the seafront. We parked and decided to go on a scavenger hunt around the town. We used a map and looked for clues starting from the seafront. We went all around the streets, through the town centre and war memorial, passing through the cemetery until we got back to the seafront. Mum bought us some fish and chips for lunch. We got out a picnic blanket and enjoyed our meal by the sea. We spent time walking along the beach. Flynn and Freddie built a sandcastle while I just lay down on the blanket soaking up the sunshine. I felt free just lying there and reflected on what life had been like over the past weeks since the lockdown. The freshness of the sea air filled my nose and it was like breathing in new life each time I filled my lungs.

The noise of people setting up close to us jolted me back to reality. I checked my phone but no messages from my friends. I got up to go for a walk, and Mum gave me some money to get ice cream for everyone. I walked along the footbridge towards the shop and watched people having fun. The sense of freedom was all around. It was as if we had travelled to a time and place where the virus did not exist. However, putting on my face mask before entering the shop brought me back to the restrictions still in place. I got the ice creams and some sweets with the change then headed back to rejoin my family. My brothers were buried in sand and mum was reading a book. The ice cream was well received, and I kicked off a conversation with mum. She spent time telling me what a lovely university town St Andrews is and how great it would be if I was to come here for university. I laughed and told her off for planning my future for me. I think Mum got the message and went back to reading.

Having spent six hours in St Andrews, it was time to go and get dad and head back to Perth. When we picked dad up, he was so relaxed and shared his golfing experience with us. I half-listened as I played on my phone. I was still on my phone when we drove into the car park near the apartment. By the time we got in, we were both refreshed and tired by the day's activities. We stayed in for the rest of the evening. Mum ordered Domino's pizza for dinner. We played a game of Cluedo before heading to bed.

For the next two days, we got up late in the mornings and explored the city centre and nearby parks. We visited Scone Palace and Huntingtower Castle. The palace and castle themselves were closed because of the virus and we could only walk around the grounds and visit the gardens. On day five of our holiday, we headed out to Crieff Hydro, a hotel with an adventure park and outdoor activities. We dropped dad off to play golf at the Crieff golf club and we went off to a day of pre-arranged adventure. We had fun on the Segway and quadbikes. The weather was so lovely that it felt as if it was telling us that the world was back to normal. We had some lunch and spent the rest of the day playing in the adventure park. It was my first time visiting the resort. Despite the social distancing rules, people were out having fun. I made some videos to post on TikTok. Mum kept an eye on Freddie as he played on the inflatables and in the kids' fort. Flynn and I were left to play on our own. Dad called to say that he was ready to be collected so we left Crieff Hydro about 5 p.m., picked him up and headed back to Perth. Dad shared his golfing experience with us again and how he did better than the game he played at St Andrews. My phone battery had died, so I had no choice but to join in the family chatter till we got back to the apartment. We went out for dinner and took a walk afterwards before heading back. My brothers watched TV while I played on my phone. Dad caught up on some work and mum continued to read her book.

I got through to Peter and Lucy and shared with them how my holiday had been going. Peter mentioned how I sounded like my usual self before the lockdown. It was at this moment that I realised how much the lockdown had affected me and how being away from home felt like much-needed therapy. The sense of freedom had a remarkable effect on me. I secretly wished it would last. Peter's family had planned to visit the Lake District during the summer holiday while Lucy was with her family visiting her grandparents in Inverness. Josh was away with his family in Belfast, and Kimberly and her parents were on vacation in Tewksbury. My friends and I were all using the time away from home to recover. From the pictures and chats we posted on Instagram it was obvious we were all having fun. Who knew that a holiday in the UK would be so precious to us! I was still chatting with my friends when dad called that it was time for bed.

The weather continued to hold up, and we spent the next two days seeing more attractions in Perth. We visited Loch Tay and Pitlochry, explored Blair Castle and climbed Kinnoull Hill. It was a wonderful experience seeing all the brilliant tourist attractions that we often overlook when we choose to go abroad for holidays.

After seven days of being in Perth and building memories from a summer holiday in lockdown, it was time to head back home. We left mid-afternoon, and as we got to Dundee, it started raining. I was so grateful that the weather had been good over the past week. The rain continued to pour until we were about ten minutes from home when it finally stopped, even though there were still dark clouds hanging in the sky. As soon as we got home and unpacked our luggage, the rain started again. Coming back home had a different feel for me compared to when we left. Gone was my caged moody spirit. The break at Perth had made me feel alive again.

The next week, Flynn and I went to tennis camp, and it was fun mixing with other kids our age. Waking up to get ready and head to camp was a challenge, though. It was difficult to get up from the cosiness of my bed, and Flynn and I often arrived at tennis camp just in time. We cycled each day as my parents thought the exercise would be great for us. That same week, the community church organised a virtual youth conference for the evenings, which Flynn and I joined. It was good to play games and listen to how everyone had coped during the lockdown.

I was sad to hear how some people had lost loved ones to the virus and had been unable to say goodbye because of the lockdown rules. Someone shared that they'd lost both their grandad and uncle within six days of each other. I could relate their experience to Peter's. All I could think about was how lucky I was compared to others.

By week three of the summer holidays, I hadn't had to talk or even hear about the virus in a while, and life almost felt normal! Well, I say normal, but of course, being restricted and people wearing masks everywhere could not be called normal. But I was so happy that I had a form of freedom and was determined to make the most of it. I'm not too sure why or how, but the restriction had made me paint and draw as a form of escape. My plan for the rest of the summer was to sleep till noon, eat breakfast while lunch was being cooked and escape back to my room to watch Netflix and draw. However, my parents had other ideas. Despite all the ways I was trying to keep myself busy, my parents did not think it was good enough. They thought it was my excuse to stay online all day, hidden in my room and being antisocial. In a sense, they were 100% correct. Yes, I was hiding in my room, avoiding house chores and being online almost all day. However, they cannot say I was antisocial if I was talking to my friends, right? I knew I was spending many hours away from my family, but which teenager in my shoes was doing anything different? This was the root cause of most of my arguments with my parents. I wanted to finish as many boxsets as I could manage before heading back to school after summer. Instead, I was often called to spend time with the family doing stuff like baking or playing board games. As if this was not enough to keep me busy, my parents then signed me up for some virtual lessons in maths, physics and chemistry, their reason being that my performance in the previous term had been below expectation. The virtual lessons were set up for three hours every week on Mondays, Wednesdays and Fridays, one hour for each subject. I was fuming, but all my promises to improve after the summer did nothing to change my parents' minds. It seemed as if they kept looking for ways to fill my days with their definition of productivity!

So, with no choice of my own, I started attending the virtual lessons. I was pleasantly surprised to find that my parents had arranged a smart young engineering graduate to deliver them. His name was Scott. He understood what I must be feeling and made the lessons fun. It was obvious that he put in a lot of effort into making the lessons enjoyable and I decided to be nice instead of difficult. I started looking forward to the lessons each week, but I did not admit this to my parents. Scott helped me to understand all the topics I had struggled with while learning in lockdown and I was glad to have this support, which continued until the week that we went back to school.

When the weather was favourable, we had mini picnics and barbecues at home. The fridge was always well stocked as my brothers and I were eating more from running around in the garden, family walks and cycling. The more active we were, the more we snacked.

Following the Scottish Government announcement that allowed two families to meet in gardens or outdoors, we finally got our first family invitation since the lockdown. A friend invited us over for a barbecue in their garden. What made this fun was that no face masks were required. We were finally socialising like normal people. At the barbecue, we ate as much as we could and had an amazing time together! Looking around us, the neighbourhood was still very quiet. I only spotted a few people in their gardens soaking up the sun or holding a barbecue. The lockdown was keeping everyone to their homes. I was not used to being at another family's home and did my best to observe the rules. I think after many weeks of restrictions, I was operating on autopilot. I am not too sure why, but this barbecue felt so different from the world around us. It was cosy with a buzz of activity. The weather was beautiful, so warm outside and the sun was shining brightly. The streets had a few children cycling and walking past but the number was so few in comparison to other summers. Most of the noise came from nearby gardens. We had so much to eat, and it tasted better being in the company of friends. I was having a great time being out of the house again, and I was not looking forward to it ending, but after three hours, we said our goodbyes and went back home. For me, it was back to Netflix.

On 30 July, the government announced that schools would be reopening. This was met with great cheer among my friends, and even my parents were relieved. For me, this was the final step towards getting back to some form of normal. This also meant it was time to start getting ready. We went to the city centre to buy school uniform and supplies. A lot had changed in the stores. The changing rooms were closed so it was difficult to try anything on – a lot of guessing was involved. We got home and thankfully found that everything fitted. Freddie was excited as he was starting his first year of primary school. It took a lot of effort to get him to take his uniform off after trying it on. There were messages from our schools to our parents every other day about preparations and steps that were being taken to make the schools safe. We were going to form year-group bubbles and teachers were going to keep giving us homework online. My friends and I chatted a lot about what to expect.

The announcement about going back to school also meant I had to focus and finish the writing tasks and music videos I had set out to do for the rest of the summer. I continued to stay in my room, and my parents stopped asking me to spend time with them. I think going back to work after the summer vacation kept them busy. Flynn had started back with his football coaching and taxiing him around had to be managed within my parents' routine. It felt like the world was catching up on time lost during lockdown to resume normal activities, like contact sports. More bubbles were being formed between households. But people began to get too comfortable and a lot of people forgot that the invisible enemy was still lurking in the shadows. Then, just like it was at the beginning of the lockdown, we started hearing about infection hotspots in the UK. Suddenly, I went from barely talking about the virus, to discussing the stringent measures being applied to contain it within the hotspots. My peace was shaken, and I was petrified that this virus was going to return with a vengeance. Each day, there was uncertainty about whether the school reopening would go ahead or not. I could not go through another lockdown. I was not sure if I would survive it. My friends and I spent more time catching up for cycling and long walks whenever we could because of the fear of being put under extreme lockdown again. When the news came through that the rate of infection had shot up in Leicester and the city had to go back under lockdown, I was petrified. I spent more time online to distract myself. I made excuses not to join the family for the BBC six o'clock news hour as I wanted my mind to be free from all the negative news. I longed for the virus to go away.

Chapter 5:

The New Normal

The world is beating the invisible enemy
A price was paid to claim this victory
Lives were lost and sacrifices were made
Many will never be the same again
Yet we live to tell the tale.

We must not lose our immediate goal
To never shut school gates again
To keep restaurants, pubs and shops open
Our sporting clubs must keep playing
If we want to live to tell the tale.

We are forever grateful to key workers
Doctors, nurses and carers
Teachers, pharmacists and postmen
Delivery drivers and shop workers
All who kept working to keep us well looked after
Just so we can live to tell the tale.

The virus may never go away
Like HIV and malaria, it may have come to stay
We must find a way to get our lives back
By defining a new normal for all humankind
In order to live to tell the tale.

After 146 days, the school gates were opened again. The government had put in a lot of effort to achieve this. Pupils like Freddie, who were starting primary school, missed out on transition days and the usual fun that accompanied it. All his transition day activities had been virtual, and I truly felt sorry for him. The transition days were important to help you understand the difference between nursery and primary school, but I guess being so young, Freddie would probably not notice the difference. I did hope this would not stop him from enjoying moving to big school. During the lockdown, he had asked me on several occasions why he would not be allowed to go to the nursery to meet his friends to say goodbye. I tried to give him an explanation about the virus, but I don't think it made sense to him.

Flynn had been enjoying his football practice and hanging out with his friends for the last three weeks of the summer, but like me, he was looking forward to going back to school and not being taught by our parents at home anymore. He seemed ready for the adventure. He was disappointed that he was not getting a chance to change the class teacher he'd had the year before, but the school thought this would make the transition to the new school year easier as the teachers would already know the abilities of the students.

I was not due back in school until Wednesday. There were a lot of emails from school to get us to understand the measures they had put in place to restrict the spread of Covid-19. We now had to wear a face mask when moving about inside the school building. One of the measures was that on gym days, we had to wear our gym kit from home and have it on all day. I shuddered at the thought of body odours that would fill the classrooms following gym sessions. Surely, this was more harmful than the risk of contracting the virus from changing clothes! Another rule was that if we chose to cycle to school, we had to do it in school uniform as the changing rooms would not be accessible. I made a mental note to avoid cycling to school until we could change! When my friends and I chatted later that evening, we all agreed cycling to school was off the table.

As I skimmed through each email, I reflected on the journey over the last five months that had brought me this moment. The virus was still out there, and some areas of the UK were struggling to keep the infection rate down. The death rate had significantly dropped, and the number of deaths recorded the day before was down to 77. To date, the total number of confirmed cases in the country was 313,798 and recorded deaths were 46,706. The thought of all the lives lost and those infected was like a record of fallen soldiers in battle.

Peter had been fine all through summer since the death of his grandad. I secretly hoped that starting school again would help all of us feel the world was getting back on its feet. I just wanted people to obey the rules so that we didn't have a second spike that could lead to another lockdown. I did not want to lose the freedom of meeting up with my friends again. Yes, the things I had taken for granted, like coming and going as I pleased, shopping without restrictions and physically going to school, had all been privileges of a normal world. I never again wanted to deal with the level of fear and anguish I'd had to work through over the past five months! I only coped by using some survival tips I had pulled together.

Let me share my survival tips for the last few months. One thing that kept me going during lockdown was thinking ahead about how it was going to change my lifestyle and being prepared. I stayed observant. If you look out for changes in rules, patterns and safety then you will know what to expect. If you are paying attention to even the minor details, you will notice the bigger details before others do. For example, if you start to notice that shopkeepers are becoming more laid back and lenient, there may be another easing of the lockdown coming. Then again, it could just be that the burden of having to keep perfectly to the rules was taking its toll.

The news and social media posts were other sources of what was going on in society. Stories of infection spikes and world crisis were everywhere. When the stories became less dramatic, the indication to me was that the virus was getting under control. These details had a massive impact on my mind. I taught myself to always have options to keep busy. I switched from drawing and painting to playing games or watching Netflix. The secret was not to get bored, so having a variety of activities was key. The family traditions, though an inconvenience sometimes, were very helpful. The baking, barbecues, homemade pizzas, Saturday brunches and walks were activities that made the days go faster in my eyes. The walks provided a break from being confined in the house. What I noticed was that whenever we went out on a walk, there were so many others out there doing the same. I guess everyone was eager to leave the house for a bit, not only me. I improved my baking skills during the lockdown, and I am proud that I can add pizza making to my resumé!

Another important factor that helped me to cope was the support network available from my friends and the community church. There is a sense of camaraderie when you are around people who are going through the same situation and thinking like you. You can work together to create fun activities to take your mind away from the events surrounding you. You can also share ideas, and, when the occasion demands, you can be vulnerable in a safe space by sharing your fears and anxieties. I would encourage everyone to check that they have a support network in place for difficult times in their lives.

I also used my passion for drawing and painting to express my feelings. I found this channel to be very effective for moments when I simply did not want social interaction. There are no walls when I am drawing or painting. I can express how much I feel without worrying about judgement, and this way, I can keep my thoughts private. For the moments when I just wanted to chill and relax, I played Roblox or binge-watched Netflix box sets. I got through *The Vampire Diaries*, *Thirteen Reasons Why*, *Beyond the Reasons*, *The Next Step* and *Never Have I Ever*, to mention just a few. When I think about it, I was busy in my way.

Yes, I coped and survived, but many did not have the same outcome that I had. They faced ruined life events, like milestone birthday celebrations and weddings. Some, like Peter, lost a loved one and have sad memories of knowing someone in the statistics of deaths due to Covid-19. There was news about a girl in our year group, Anna, whose parents had separated during the lockdown. I felt sorry for Anna, as living in a house with your parents fighting must have left her crushed emotionally. A lot of families struggled to co-exist during the proximity of lockdown. I overheard my parents talking about the impact of furloughing and job losses on families. The everyday news kept us updated about long-term establishments going out of business. The economic landscape of the world was deeply impacted by the pandemic. Even airlines were grounded for months. Dad, who usually travelled a lot for work, was one of the flying customers forced to stay at home.

One thing did catch the attention of the world during the lockdown. This was the Black Lives Matter movement. The brutal killing of Blacks in America by police officers made headline news. George Floyd's death, and others that followed, made the world stop and think about racism and equality. The debates and protests have continued to this day. In a twisted way, the oppression and injustice from racism finally got global attention because the world was at a standstill and was forced to listen. I think my generation was not aware of the injustice and inequality in race until the lockdown. Josh and Lucy said we should join one of the protests, but when we mentioned it to our parents, they were strongly against the idea. My parents said actions in our day-to-day lives are more powerful ways of making a difference. I was not surprised by their response!

As I got dressed for school on Wednesday, I realised that the world I was stepping out into had changed. The way things were before the lockdown was now gone and adaptations were being made to keep on living with the invisible enemy. As the virus was being managed by social distancing rules, scientists across the world were working hard to create a vaccine, with the University of Oxford leading the research work in the UK. Clinical trials to make sure it is effective and does not produce adverse side effects has delayed any release. As with anything else that has to do with the pandemic, there have been a lot of conspiracy theories about the vaccine and how it represents the end of time. It was apparent that being cooped up at home for five months had made human thinking go into overdrive! My friends and I took a rational approach to a vaccine. It was to protect us until the virus could be eradicated, like smallpox. Without a vaccine, the world will have to continue to maintain social distancing and the wearing of face masks, which is already becoming a struggle judging by the news of spikes in infection rates in areas across Britain.

The excitement of going back into the classroom and a desire to leave the house and join my friends overcame my thoughts. I went downstairs, and after a quick breakfast of toast and jam with a few sips of water, I left the house. I met up with Lucy and we walked to a nearby park where Kimberly, Josh and Peter were waiting for us. This was our usual meet-up point before school. As we walked, we chatted about what the first day back would feel like. I joked about how the teachers would try and keep their distance. I silently hoped that anyone with a cough or a cold would just stay at home to avoid us all going into two weeks of isolation.

It was five minutes to nine when we reached the school gates. No one was allowed into the building until the bell rang, and we all had to enter the school through designated doors for each year group. This was part of the safety measures put in place. As I stood with my friends a sense of gratitude washed over me. Each of us had been affected by the virus, but we were all still here. The lockdown had taught us to be grateful for the simple things in life. Indoor activities, like swimming, church gatherings and large parties, might still be banned, and no spectators were allowed at sports events, like football matches, but even with these restrictions in place, we were back at school and could walk and roam freely, albeit with caution. Shops were open and some international flights had resumed. My parents, though still working from home, still had their jobs. We had relearnt the value of being together as a family and feeling safe. I had been through the greatest emotional roller-coaster of my life and learnt to survive the lockdown. I believe this experience has prepared me to cope with whatever crises life may throw at me in the future.

As the bell rang, I put on my face mask and walked in. The fresh smell of disinfectant filled my nose. The hand sanitiser by the door had to be used before proceeding any further. I could tell that the school was doing everything it could to make it a virus-free environment. My first class for the day was biology. I recalled that this was the last class I'd had before the lockdown and chuckled. Lucy, Peter and I were in the same biology group. As part of managing the spread of the virus, we had maintained the same classes and groups as the previous school year. Mr Appleton, our biology teacher, stood in front of the class and went over the social distancing rules. We are now expected to learn using our laptops instead of textbooks. The topic for the day was cells and organisation. I was intrigued to see the application of the topic to the virus that had brought the world to its knees.

There I was, sitting in class and thinking about the day the restrictions would end, and when hugging people without much thought would be normal again. I looked forward to the day when the coronavirus would be a disease confined to the laboratory. I missed the version of the world before the virus. I yearned for the ability to share food with my friends and hang out indoors to watch a movie. I craved the freedom that once was but no longer existed. For now, I was left to make do with the present and be satisfied with being counted as a survivor of the coronavirus pandemic.

Printed in Great Britain
by Amazon